30°E
60°
90°
120°
150°
Arctic Ocean
EUROPE
ASIA
AFRICA
Pacific Ocean
Indian Ocean
AUSTRALIA
ANTARCTICA

Countries of the World

Cuba

Jen Green

Damián Fernández and Alejandro de la Fuente, Consultants

NATIONAL GEOGRAPHIC
WASHINGTON, D.C.

Contents

Foreword

The Arawak natives who lived in Cuba at the time the Europeans arrived in 1492 must have looked at them with worry and fear. As the Spanish conquest of the island went ahead, European diseases and fighting killed off huge numbers of people. In only decades the original inhabitants of Cuba, the largest island in the Antilles, had been virtually wiped out. So began European "civilization" in Cuba.

The natives were replaced with slaves brought from almost all parts of Africa, from Senegal in the north to Angola in the south. The slaves built cities, worked in mining and agriculture, and produced the riches that made Cuba a wealthy colony. Travelers can still appreciate this wealth in the beautiful colonial mansions of Havana and Trinidad, or in the forts that guard the harbors of Havana and Santiago de Cuba. But it is important to remember that this wealth was created by thousands of enslaved laborers, forcibly taken from their families and communities.

European colonialism left other marks on the island and its inhabitants. It was from the interactions among natives, various Africans, and Spaniards that Cuban culture and the Cuban people were created. The lively Cuban culture that is known around the world rests precisely on these different influences.

Creating a nation that would include these groups was a long and hard process. The involvement of foreign powers made the process of building an independent nation even more difficult, for Cuba remained a colony of Spain until 1898 and was then occupied by American forces. The United States exercised considerable influence over Cuba until the revolution of 1959 that brought Fidel Castro to power. This revolution changed the lives of Cubans in significant ways and has been opposed by

the United States—Cuba's biggest neighbor—for more than forty years. At first, the revolutionary government enjoyed widespread support from the people. Workers and the poorest members of society benefited from new programs in nutrition, free medical care, and education. But many Cubans now resent the limitations on their civil and political rights.

▲ A father and his young son prepare to do the day's grocery shopping in a street in old Havana.

Alejandro de la Fuente
University of Pittsburgh

An Island Nation

THE CARIBBEAN ISLANDS are well known for their sandy beaches. With a coastline more than twice as long as that of California, Cuba has more beaches than anywhere else in the Caribbean.

A day at the beach for a Cuban is a little different than what you might expect. The shores of most Caribbean islands are filled with hotels, marinas, and other facilities for tourists. But much of Cuba's coastline is empty, untouched and unchanged for many years.

Cuba's shoreline has more than just beaches. The island's waters have some of the largest coral reefs in the Caribbean, and in places its coast gives way to crocodile-infested swamps and lagoons. The cliffs are filled with caves formed by centuries of crashing waves and there are many hidden inlets—hideaways once used by pirates, rebel soldiers, and runaway slaves.

◀ **A horse and rider trot through the surf of a Cuban beach.**

WHAT'S THE WEATHER LIKE?

Lying close to the Tropic of Cancer, Cuba has a warm, dry climate. There are variations across the island, however. Coastal areas are cooler than areas inland, while the mountains are so cold they occasionally experience frosts.

Most rain falls from May to October, when thunderstorms are common. In late summer and fall hurricanes may damage crops and force thousands to flee their homes for safety. The map opposite shows the physical features of Cuba. Labels on this map and similar maps throughout this book identify many places pictured in each chapter.

Average Temperature & Rainfall

Average High/Low Temperatures; Yearly Rainfall

Pinar del Río Norte
86° F (30° C) / 68° F (20° C); 39 in (99 cm)

Havana
84° F (29° C) / 68° F (20° C); 39 in (99 cm)

Varadero
83° F (28° C) / 68° F (20° C); 39 in (99 cm)

Manzanillo
86° F (30° C) / 73° F (23° C); 13 in (34 cm)

Guantánamo
87° F (31° C) / 74° F (24° C); 13 in (34 cm)

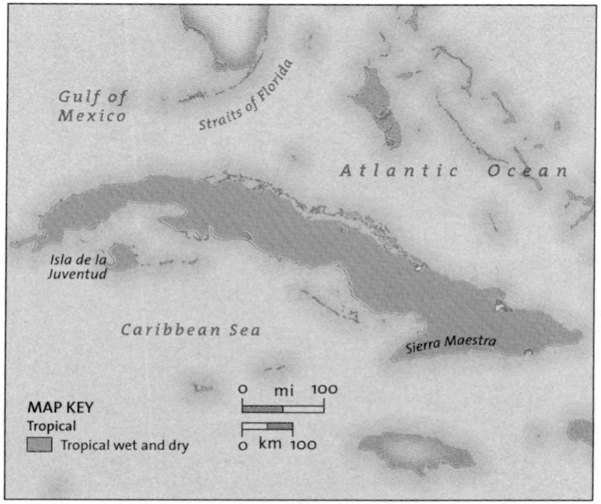

FAST FACTS

Official name: Republic of Cuba
Form of government: Socialist republic
Capital: Havana
Population: 11,382,820
Official language: Spanish
Currency: Peso and convertible peso
Area: 42,802 square miles (110,860 square kilometers)
Bordering nations: U.S. naval base at Guantánamo Bay
Highest point: Pico Turquino 6,578 feet (2,005 meters)
Lowest point: Sea level 0 feet (0 meters)
Major mountain ranges: Sierra de los Órganos, Sierra del Rosario, Sierra del Escambray, Sierra Maestra
Major rivers: Cauto (longest: 230 miles; 370 kilometers), Salado, Guantánamo, Sevilla, Saramaguacán
Largest lake: Leche Lagoon 26 square miles (67 square kilometers)
Coastline: 2,075 miles (3,735 kilometers)

Physical Map
Gulf of Mexico
STATES
Straits of Florida
BAHAMAS
North America
Atlantic Ocean
CUBA
Pacific Ocean
South America
TROPIC OF CANCER
STREET SCENE, page 1 AND FATHER AND SON, page 5
ZAPATA SWAMP, page 13
Havana
Varadero
Matanzas
Archipiélago de Sabana
Atlantic Ocean
Archipiélago de los Colorados
2,293 ft
699 m
Sierra de los Órganos
Sierra del Rosario
Viñales Valley
Pinar del Río
Golfo de Batabanó
Zapata Swamp
Bahía Guadiana
Yucatan Channel
Nueva Gerona
Isla de la Juventud
Archipiélago de los Canarreos
Cayo Largo
Cienfuegos
C U B A
Sagua la Grande
Santa Clara
Archipiélago de Camagüey
Cayo Coco
3,740 ft
1,140 m
Sierra del Escambray
Sancti Spíritus
Morón
Laguna de Leche
ROCK FORMATIONS, page 11 AND HONEYCOMB CAVE, page 12
LOS COCOS BEACH, page 2, 6
FARMLAND, page 10
Camagüey
Golfo de Ana María
San Pedro
Las Tunas
Holguín
Bahía de Nipe
Archipiélago de los Jardines de la Reina
Manzanillo
Cauto
Bayamo
Golfo de Guacanayabo
Sierra Maestra
Guantánamo
Pico Turquino
(Highest point in Cuba)
6,578 ft
2,005 m
Santiago de Cuba
U.S. NAVAL BASE GUANTANAMO BAY
Windward Passage
Caribbean Sea
Cayman Islands (U.K.)
Grand Cayman
MAP KEY
National capital
Selected city
Elevation
0 miles 100
0 km 100
JAMAICA
HAITI

▲ **Cuba's flat lowland areas are used as farmland, while thick forests grow on the steep mountainsides.**

Birth of an Island

Cuba is the largest island in the Caribbean Sea. It is similar in area to the state of Pennsylvania. The nearest countries are the Bahamas, Haiti, and Jamaica. But its most important neighbor is the United States. The southern tip of Florida lies just 90 miles (145 km) to the north. The Straits of Florida between the two nations can be dangerous for sailors, even on modern boats. A strong ocean current runs through it from the Gulf of Mexico, and there are frequent storms.

Cuba and its neighbors form the Greater Antilles island chain. These islands, which also include Puerto Rico, were created millions of years ago by a collision between two of the immense rocky plates that make up Earth's crust. As the Caribbean and North American plates drove into each other, the seabed buckled upward, broke the surface, and formed the islands.

A Jewel in the Ocean

Cuba is long and narrow. It stretches 750 miles (1,200 km) from east to west, but is less than 60 miles (100 km) wide in most places. On a map, Cuba looks like a giant alligator swimming east, with a long tail curving into the Gulf of Mexico.

THE MOGOTES

The Viñales Valley at the western tip of Cuba looks like nowhere else on the island—and like few places on Earth. Above the fields rise small, rounded rocky hills. These so-called mogotes are the remains of a limestone plateau that formed beneath the sea over 40 million years ago and was pushed upward to become land. As rainwater wore away the soft limestone, the rain hollowed out caves and channels beneath the plateau. Eventually the limestone collapsed and crumbled away. The pillars of harder rock that remained formed the mogotes. The hills are a popular challenge for local rock climbers.

▲ Mogotes rise above the mist in the Viñales Valley. The thick vegetation of each mogote has its own unique community of wildlife.

CUBA'S CAVE SYSTEM

The limestone hills of western Cuba are full of caverns and underground rivers. The Sierra de los Órganos have several spectacular caves, including Santo Tomas, the largest system on Cuba. Its five levels of caverns run for 25 miles (44 km). The nearby Cueva del Indio was once occupied by native peoples; they used it to hide from Spanish invaders. The Cueva de los Cimarrones was also a hideout, this time for runaway African slaves. *Cimarron* means "slave" in Spanish.

▲ **Honeycomb Cave near Viñales, where fossils of extinct animals that were unique to Cuba have been unearthed**

The main island is surrounded by many smaller islands—up to four thousand, depending on how many of the small ones you count. Only a few of the smaller islands have people living on them.

High and Low

High mountains and rolling hills cover about a third of the island. Eastern Cuba has several lofty ranges, including the Sierra Maestra—the "Teacher Mountains," which rise up along the southern coast. This range includes the island's highest point, Pico Turquino. In the west rise the Sierra de los Órganos—"the Organ Mountains." They were named by Spanish sailors who came to Cuba in about 1500. They thought the tall, rocky peaks resembled the pipes of church organs.

Two-thirds of Cuba are lowland plains. The largest flat area is in the center of the island. Almost all of the lowlands are used for farming. The plains are covered in orchards and fields of sugarcane, Cuba's most important export. Cuba's warm climate makes it a good place for growing tropical fruits, such as mangoes and pineapples.

Water Everywhere

Cuba can be quite damp, especially in the rainy season, from May to October. More than 600 rivers and streams drain the hills. Most are fairly short. The longest river, the Cauto, flows for only 230 miles (370 km) in the southeast. On a peninsula—land with the ocean on three sides—in the west of Cuba, streams feed the Zapata Swamp, the largest wetland in the Caribbean. The swamp is one of the world's most important wildlife reserves, with rare Cuban crocodiles and birds that live nowhere else.

▲ **The Zapata Swamp is a shallow wetland. Much of it is protected as the Zapata Biosphere Reserve. The wetland is home to the Cuban crocodile, one of the world's rarest crocodiles.**

Natural Harbors

Cuba was one of the first American places to be discovered by Europeans. Christopher Columbus sighted the island on his famous voyage in 1492. Cuba soon lay at the heart of important sea routes from the Gulf of Mexico to Europe and Africa. Inlets along Cuba's coast, such as the site of the capital, Havana, make fine harbors. The inlets of the smaller islands were hiding places for pirates who raided Spanish galleons carrying treasure from the Americas back to Europe.

A MILKY LAGOON

Leche Lagoon (Milk Lagoon) near Morón is Cuba's largest lake, covering 26 square miles (67 sq km). Many tourists visit to see the white water that gave it its name. The milky color is created by white calcium carbonate powder on the lake bed, which is churned up by tides flowing through channels between the lake and the sea to the north. Carp and pike swim in the semi-salty water, while herons and flamingoes feed along the shore.

Unique Wildlife

IN THE LUSH FORESTS OF CUBA, small, brightly colored creatures dart through the air. It would be easy to mistake them for large insects. Wasps that size might have quite a nasty sting. In fact, the creatures are harmless. Bee hummingbirds are the world's smallest bird: just 2 inches (5 cm) long and weighing less than a penny.

Like other hummingbirds, this one sips nectar from flowers without landing on the plant. Instead the bird hovers in midair, beating its wings 200 times a second. The sound made by the wingbeats gave the bird its name: It sounds like the buzzing of bees. The Cubans also call the bird *zunzuncito*, or "little buzzer." This tiny bird is just one of many unique Cuban species, which also include the world's smallest frog.

◀ Cuba's bee hummingbird, the world's smallest bird, must drink eight times its own weight in water each day or it will dry out and die.

AMAZING VARIETY

For a small island, Cuba has many different habitats. There are mountain forests, lush jungles, grasslands, and even pockets of desert. Along the coast, the habitats include swamps, mangroves, coral reefs, and many small, low-lying coral islands called cays (pronounced "kees"). The map opposite shows the main habitats found on Cuba. These many habitats are home to thousands of plants and animals that are found only on Cuba. The unique species include around 90 percent of Cuba's reptiles, 30 of its 180 butterfly species, and almost half of the plants growing on the island.

▶ **Painted snails are unique to Cuba. Legend has it that the snail's colorful swirls were painted using yellow from the sun, white from the surf, and black from the night.**

Species at Risk

Cuba's wildlife is under threat from several sources. Many of the island's forest habitats have been felled to provide timber or firewood, and to make way for fields. Larger animals were hunted for food, while the island's crocodiles were killed for their skins. Some Cuban animals have become rare because they are being hunted by predators such as cats and dogs, brought to the island by settlers. Several species have become extinct, including a giant running owl and a ground sloth. Cuba's habitats and rare creatures are now protected in reserves that cover 20 percent of the island.

Species at risk include:

- West Indian manatee
- Cuban solenodon (mammal)
- Cuban crocodile
- American crocodile
- Painted snail
- Cuban pygmy owl
- Ivory-billed woodpecker

Vegetation & Ecosystems Map
UNITED STATES
Gulf of Mexico
Straits of Florida
BAHAMAS
TROPIC OF CANCER
Atlantic Ocean
Havana
Matanzas
Archipiélago de Sabana
Archipiélago de Camagüey
Archipiélago de los Colorados
Sierra de los Órganos
Viñales N.P.
Pinar del Río
Bahía Guadiana
Yucatán Channel
Golfo de Batabanó
Ciénaga de Zapata N.P.
Cienfuegos
Sagua la Grande
Santa Clara
Sierra del Escambray
Sancti Spíritus
Archipiélago de los Canarreos
Isla de la Juventud
Cayo Largo
Camagüey
Golfo de Ana María
San Pedro
Archipiélago de los Jardines de la Reina
Las Tunas
Holguín
Cauto
Golfo de Guacanayabo
Pico Cristal N.P.
Alejandro de Humboldt N.P.
Guantánamo
Windward Passage
Sierra Maestra
Desembarco del Granma N.P.
Turquino N.P.
Santiago de Cuba
U.S. NAVAL BASE GUANTANAMO BAY
Caribbean Sea
Cayman Islands (U.K.)
Hispaniola
HAITI
JAMAICA
MAP KEY
Primary Vegetation Zones/Ecosystems
Flooded grasslands
Mangroves
Tropical and subtropical coniferous forests
Tropical and subtropical dry broadleaf forests
Tropical and subtropical moist broadleaf forests
Protected Lands
Selected national parks and national reserves
0 miles 100
0 km 100

In the Forest

A few centuries ago, rain forests covered almost all of Cuba. Now most of the lowland forests have been cleared to make way for sugar plantations, fields, orchards, and pastures for cattle. Pockets of rain forest survive in the east of the country and in upland areas that are too rugged for farming. Since the 1960s Cubans have been replanting trees to create new forests of palms, pines, and broad-leaved trees.

Palm trees are everywhere, but some of Cuba's most interesting native trees are much more unusual. Roots trail down from the branches of the banyan tree to the ground, where they form new trunks. The same tree can have dozens of trunks. The roots of the jaguey grow out of its trunk above the ground. Another species, the cork palm, is an example of what

TREE OF LEGEND

The ceiba is one of Cuba's tallest trees, growing about 200 feet (60 m) high. It is also one of the most useful. Its seeds are wrapped in a mass of silk fibers called kapok. This soft material, which is also known as tree cotton, is used to stuff cushions and pad chairs. But the ceiba also has a spiritual reputation. It is part of many Cuban legends, and is sacred to the followers of Santería. Followers of this Cuban religion believe that the tree forms a pathway between Earth and the heavens for *orishas*, or spirits. Worshipers place offerings around the tree's roots.

▲ A tall ceiba tree is supported by buttress roots that stick out from the trunk.

scientists call a "living fossil." The prehistoric plant has existed in the same form for 100 million years.

Beneath the canopy (covering of leaves and branches), the forests are green and shady places. There are bright flashes of color from flowers, such as orchids and hibiscus, and birds. They include the *tocororo*, Cuba's national bird. Its red, white, and blue plumage matches the Cuban flag.

▲ **Orchids bloom in a Cuban forest. There are about 100 orchid species that are unique to the island.**

The green and blue *cotorra*, or Cuban parrot, also lives in the forests. In the past, the species was at risk of extinction as farmers destroyed its habitat. Today the parrots again have a future—about 10,000 birds now live in protected areas.

◀ **A manatee swims in shallow water. These gentle vegetarians use their flexible lips to pull up water plants for food, and their flippers to dig up roots.**

Coastal Community

Many legends surround the manatee, a mammal that swims in the mouths of Cuba's rivers. The Spaniards who first saw them are said to have mistaken them for mermaids, with human bodies and the tails of fish.

Around the coast, the tides flood low-lying areas of mangrove trees. Their stilt-like roots are covered at high tide but exposed at low tide. The shallows contain fish, turtles, and crabs, which attract wading birds such as flamingos, spoonbills, and egrets.

Cuba's warm coastal waters are ideal for coral reefs, which are the ocean's richest habitat. The reefs are home to a range of wildlife from tiny angelfish to sharks and barracuda. The larger fish are popular with sportfishers.

Swamp Creature

The isolated Zapata Swamp is home to the Cuban crocodile. This expert killer hunts fish, turtles, mammals—and birds. It uses its strong tail to leap out of the water to grab birds from overhanging branches. At over 12 feet (3.5 m) long, the crocodile is Cuba's largest native animal. Its numbers have fallen because of hunting and because many swamps have been drained to create farmland. The Cuban government now breeds the crocs in farms and then releases them into the wild to keep them from extinction.

▲ The Cuban crocodile is one of the rarest crocodile species in the world. It survives only in two swamps in Cuba—Zapata and Lanier Swamp on the Isle of Youth.

Only in Cuba

▲ The Cuban solenodon is one of the most unusual mammals in the world. The only other surviving species of solenodon lives on Hispaniola, an island east of Cuba made up of Haiti and the Dominican Republic.

Experts believe that about 900 animals are unique to Cuba and its islands. The ancient ancestors of these animals reached Cuba from other places. Some swam; insects, bats, and birds flew or were blown along by strong winds. Land animals arrived on floating clumps of vegetation. Once on Cuba, the animals evolved (changed) to suit their new habitats—and completely new species emerged.

Mammals that live only on Cuba include the solenodon, a large relative of shrews with small eyes and a tail as long as its body. This rare creature hunts at night, poking its long, flexible snout into holes to sniff out insects. The ratlike hutia is much more common. Hutias will eat anything, especially garbage in villages and towns.

Cuba is home to the smallest species of bat in the Americas. The butterfly bat weighs a fraction of an ounce, and its wingspan (distance between the tips of each wing) is just 5 inches (12 cm). The world's smallest frog also lives on Cuba, in the eastern rain forests. It's not surprising that it was not discovered until 1990: The adult frogs are no bigger than a dime.

Centuries of Change

THE MIGHTY WALLS of El Morro Castle at the entrance to Havana's harbor are a reminder of Cuba's turbulent past. The arrival of the Taino people from Venezuela several hundred years ago was the start of a series of upheavals. Then followed a brutal invasion by Spanish troops in 1511. French pirates attacked the Spanish colony, and British troops occupied Havana for a year in the 1700s, using El Morro itself as their stronghold. In 1898, American forces helped to end Spanish rule. And in 1956, a force of Cubans under Fidel Castro landed from Mexico to start the revolution that would lead to Cuba becoming a communist state. The fight for Cuba has been a long one because the country can control the shipping routes across the Caribbean.

◄ El Morro Castle is located at the entrance to Havana's harbor. It was built in the 1590s to protect the city from pirates.

CENTURIES OF CHANGE

Cuba's original inhabitants were the Ciboney and Guanahatabey people. About one thousand years ago, the Taino, farming people from what is now Venezuela, started to take over the island. By the time Columbus arrived in the late 15th century, the Taino ruled most of the island.

In 1511, a Spanish force defeated the Taino easily. The Spanish chose sites for seven new cities: Baracoa, Bayamo, Trinidad, Sancti Spiritus, Puerto Principe (now named Camagüey), Santiago, and Havana; and they ruled Cuba for 388 years. By 1902, Cuba had finally become independent, but it was governed by rulers heavily influenced by the United States. Then, in 1959 revolutionaries took control, making the island fully independent. They have been in power ever since.

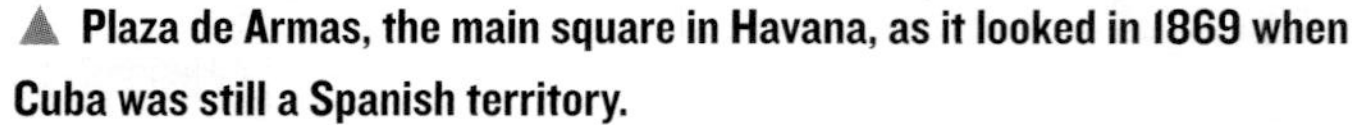

▲ **Plaza de Armas, the main square in Havana, as it looked in 1869 when Cuba was still a Spanish territory.**

Time line

This chart shows the dates of important events in the history of Cuba.

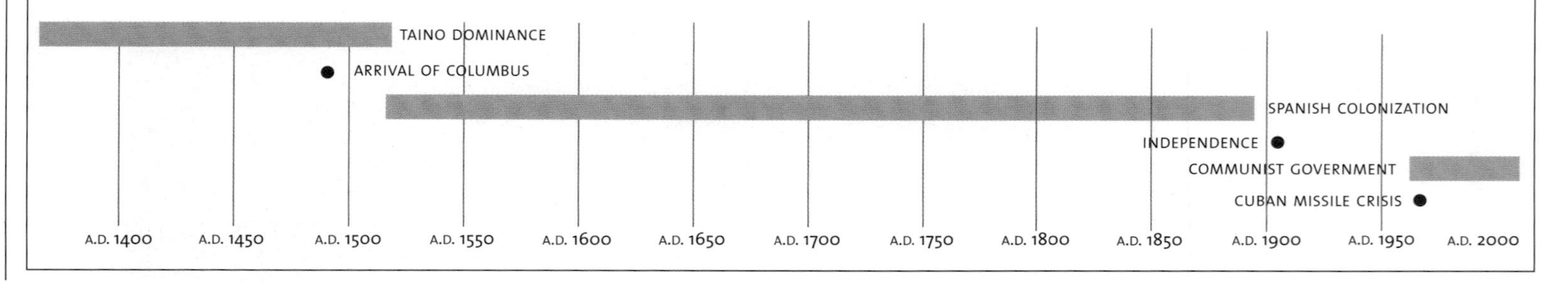

Historical Map
Slave trade route to New Orleans
UNITED STATES
Gulf of Mexico
Straits of Florida
BAHAMAS
Atlantic
Ocean
TROPIC OF CANCER
EL MORRO CASTLE, page 2, 22 AND PLAZA DE ARMAS, page 24, AND JOSÉ MARTÍ MEMORIAL, page 29
Havana
CUBA
Sancti Spiritus
Trinidad
TOWN SQUARE, page 28
Puerto Principe (Camagüey)
PRISONERS, BAY OF PIGS, page 32
MISSILE BASE, page 33
Bayamo
Santiago de Cuba
Baracoa
FIDEL CASTRO, (BIRTHPLACE), page 31
REFUGEE CAMP, GUANTANAMO BAY, page 30
HAITI
DOMINICAN REPUBLIC
Hispaniola
PUERTO RICO
JAMAICA
Slave trade route from Central Africa
Slave trade route from West Africa
Caribbean Sea
HONDURAS
NICARAGUA
MAP KEY
Spanish territory, 1535
First Spanish settlements
Columbus's first voyage, 1492–3
Columbus's second voyage, 1493–6
Slave routes
Present-day boundaries and country names are shown.
0 miles 200
0 km 200

A Spanish Colony

The explorer Christopher Columbus claimed Cuba for Spain on his first voyage to the Americas in 1492. It was nearly twenty years later that 300 Spaniards settled at Baracoa, hoping to find gold. They failed but began making use of other resources, digging mines and clearing land for plantations. They enslaved the native people (mainly Taino), thousands of whom died from harsh treatment. However, far more natives died from European diseases such as smallpox. There may have been 100,000 Cubans in 1492. Fifty years later, only a few thousand were left. Today, the closest descendants of the native peoples live near Baracoa.

By the mid-1500s Cuba had become a key stop on the route between Spain and its colonies in South and Central America, where there was plenty of gold and

PEOPLE OF A CENTRAL PLACE

Before the Spanish arrived, Cuba was home to three major peoples: the Guanahatabey, Ciboney, and Taino. The Guanahatabey were gatherers who lived on fruits and roots, while the Ciboney were hunters and fishers. Both were living on Cuba by 1,000 B.C. The Taino arrived from South America around A.D. 800. They were farmers who grew beans and maize in the east of the island. It was probably the Taino who gave Cuba its name: Cubanacan, which means "a central place."

The Taino put up a fight when the Spanish arrived in 1511. A chief named Hatuey led a rebellion, but with little success. He was captured and burned at the stake. Today, Hatuey is regarded as Cuba's first national hero.

▲ The Taino made this stone carving, or *cemi,* before the arrival of the Spanish. Cemis represent the spirits of ancestors. They have been found on islands throughout the Caribbean.

▲ **Slaves brought from Africa work harvesting sugarcane in the 19th century. The cane would be taken to the mill in the background to be processed into sugar and syrup.**

silver. Treasure ships sailing for Spain stopped off at Havana to prepare for the voyage across the Atlantic Ocean. The settlement grew into a major port.

Sugar and Slaves

Ships sailing from Havana also carried a cargo that was sometimes called "white gold": sugar. Columbus had brought sugarcane to the Caribbean, where it grew rapidly. Spanish plantation owners made fortunes, but their workers were slaves. After native Cubans virtually died out, the Spaniards imported enslaved Africans. The slaves survived just an average seven years in the terrible conditions. The Spaniards imported more and more slaves to Cuba: about 1.3 million in 300 years. By the middle of the 19th century there were 500,000 Africans in Cuba, half the total population, and the island produced a third of the world's sugar.

The Struggle for Independence

Most of Spain's colonies had become independent in the 1820s, but Cuba remained under Spanish rule. Many Cubans wanted change: They resisted Spanish authority and wanted independence. But wealthy slave owners feared that independence might spark a slave rebellion, as had happened in neighboring Haiti in the 1790s. Instead, they wanted Cuba to join the United States, where slavery was still legal, so their plantation businesses could continue working. However, this option vanished when slavery was abolished in the United States in 1865.

In 1868, a landowner named Carlos Manuel de Céspedes freed his slaves and began a war against Spanish troops in Cuba. Although Céspedes was killed, the fighting lasted until 1878, when the Spaniards made a peace deal. Cuba would still be a colony, but any slaves who had fought in the war

SPANISH HERITAGE: TRINIDAD

The beautiful city of Trinidad reflects Cuba's history as a Spanish colony. This port on the southern coast, founded in 1514, grew rich as a trading center for sugar and slaves. Wealthy businessmen built fine mansions and beautiful Spanish-style churches around its main square. Few new buildings were constructed after 1900, so the town kept its colonial character. In the late 20th century, the old town was carefully restored. It is now a tourist attraction. In 1988, the United Nations made Trinidad a World Heritage site.

▲ This square in Trinidad has changed little since the days of the Spanish colony.

JOSÉ MARTÍ

Poet José Martí (1853–1895) was a key leader of the Cuban independence movement. As a young man, Martí was imprisoned for supporting independence, and then sent to live abroad. He spent time in Spain, the United States, and in many parts of Central America. While working as a journalist in New York City, Martí continued to campaign for Cuban independence. He founded the Cuban Revolutionary Party in 1892 and was the mastermind behind the Second War of Independence (1895–1898). Martí returned to Cuba for the war but was killed on the first day of fighting. Martí's writings fill 70 books, but he is probably most famous for writing the words that are used in the song "Guantanamera," Cuba's unofficial anthem.

José Martí's memorial in Havana houses a museum about his life.

would be allowed to go free. Slavery was finally abolished in Cuba in 1886.

In 1895, the Cuban Revolutionary Party began a second war against the Spanish. The United States sent a warship, the USS *Maine*, to protect Americans living in Cuba. In 1898, the *Maine* blew up in Havana harbor. The explosion was likely an accident, but some Americans wanted to go to war to force the Spaniards out of the region. The U.S. government chose to blame the explosion on the Spaniards and entered the war on the side of the rebels. Spain was soon defeated.

Cuba was still not fully independent, however. The island was placed under U.S. protection for a period of 30 years. Cubans had their own constitution, but it gave the U.S. government a say in Cuban affairs.

Dictators and Domination

By the 1930s, Cuban politicians no longer had to answer to the U.S. government, but U.S. companies owned most of Cuba's industry. Although the sugar industry prospered, and Havana became a leading tourist destination, much of Cuba's income went to the

A CORNER OF THE UNITED STATES

Not all of Cuba belongs to the Cubans. Near the eastern tip of the island, Guantánamo Bay is home to a U.S. naval base. The United States took over the bay in 1902, when the rest of Cuba became independent. After the revolution of 1959, relations between the two powers became hostile, and the base was heavily fortified. It is protected by the world's largest minefield (area of hidden bombs).

This little corner of the United States has supermarkets, a TV station, and even its own McDonald's. In 2002, the base became the location for a prison for suspected terrorists. Guantánamo was chosen because it was thought not to be covered by the U.S. laws about keeping prisoners and holding trials.

▲ In the mid-1990s some 50,000 refugees fleeing political unrest in the country of Haiti lived in tents at Guantánamo Bay.

United States. Meanwhile, Cuban politics were corrupt and unstable. In 1933, a soldier named Fulgencio Batista seized power. Batista controlled Cuba for most of the next 25 years, despite being driven abroad for a time. Batista used violence and corruption to stay in power.

▲ **Fidel Castro (left) and Che Guevara pictured in 1960, not long after taking power in Cuba. Castro has been president of Cuba ever since. Guevara left Cuba in 1965 to lead other revolutions in Africa and then Bolivia. He was killed by the Bolivian army in 1967.**

Revolution

In 1953, a lawyer named Fidel Castro (1926–) led an attack on a Cuban army base, hoping to spark a rebellion against the government. The attack failed, and most of Castro's 160 men died. Castro was exiled to Mexico, where he met an Argentine revolutionary named Ernesto "Che" Guevara. In 1956 they returned to Cuba with a small force to try again. Batista's soldiers defeated the rebels, but Castro, his brother Raúl, and Guevara escaped with a small band to the Sierra Maestra in eastern Cuba. For three years, the mountains became the base for sneak attacks against Batista's forces. More Cubans joined the rebels, and their attacks caused more damage. On January 1, 1959, Batista fled. Castro took control. His 800 fighters had defeated an army of 30,000 men.

At first, the U.S. government agreed to work with Castro, but relations soon became less friendly. Castro

A FAILED INVASION

Soon after Fidel Castro took control of Cuba in 1959, the United States began planning to remove him from power. U.S. intelligence agencies began to train a small army of anti-Castro Cubans who had fled their homeland after the revolution.

In April 1961, President John F. Kennedy gave the go-ahead for the anti-Castro force to invade. Using U.S. equipment, the rebel army landed at the Bay of Pigs on the southern coast.

Castro's army easily outnumbered the invaders, who did not make it far inland. Within four days the fighting was over. More than 1,000 invaders were captured. The United States agreed to give Cuba $53 million worth of food and medicine in return for the prisoners' release.

▲ Rebels captured during the failed invasion at the Bay of Pigs are led away under armed guard.

put all U.S.-owned factories under state control. In return, the United States banned all trade with Cuba. Cuba began trading with the communist Soviet Union, which was engaged in a tense struggle with the United States for strategic influence around the world. This lengthy conflict was known as the Cold War because the two sides did not actually fight each other. The United States saw Cuba's alliance with the Soviets as a threat. The island became a flashpoint that threatened to spark the Cold War into all-out fighting.

Missile Crisis

Hundreds of thousands of Cubans opposed to Castro fled to the United States. In 1961, the U.S. government backed a force of exiles in an invasion of Cuba. The operation was a disaster, but it worried Castro. He secretly set up bases with Soviet nuclear missiles. When U.S. aircraft spotted the bases in 1962, President John F. Kennedy

threatened war unless the missiles were removed. For a few days it seemed the world was on the brink of nuclear conflict. At the last moment, the Soviets gave in. They removed the missiles in return for a promise that the United States would not invade Cuba.

▲ **A photograph taken by a U.S. spy plane shows a missile base being built on Cuba in 1962. Missiles fired from Cuba could have hit U.S. cities without warning.**

Uneasy Neighbors

The world has changed a lot since 1959. Castro lost his major supporter with the breakup of the Soviet Union in 1991. He was forced to make changes to improve the Cuban economy and keep the country going. However, relations between the United States and Cuba were still frosty at the start of the 21st century. The U.S. ban on trade with Cuba continues, and Castro is still in power, but he is in poor health, creating uncertainty about the future.

A Melting Pot of Cultures

IN MOST OF THE WORLD, carnival occurs in early spring, just before Lent, the somber period leading up to Easter in the Roman Catholic tradition. But in Cuba, carnival is celebrated in July to mark the anniversary of Fidel Castro's first rebellion in 1953. Cuba has no official religion, and today only about one in ten Cubans are Catholics. But though Cuban carnivals are no longer about religion, the streets are still packed for carnival with people dancing to lively music.

All year round, it seems as if bands are everywhere in parts of Havana as their music spills onto the streets. Like Cuba's food, language, arts, and customs, its music reflects the country's past. It has influences from Cuba's time as a Spanish colony and from over a million Africans who arrived as slaves.

◀ **A brightly costumed dancer makes her way through the streets during a summer carnival in Santiago de Cuba, a city in southern Cuba.**

CUBA'S PEOPLE

In July 2006, Cuba had an estimated population of 11,382,820. That figure marks a recovery from a big drop in population after the revolution of 1959, when hundreds of thousands of opponents of the new government moved abroad. Cuba's population has increased slowly compared to that of its neighbors, however. Many thousands of people still leave the country every year. The rise in population is due in part to Cuba's health-care system. Cubans live for an average of 77 years, and babies are born more often than people die.

People of mixed race make up 51 percent of the population; 37 percent are white, 11 percent are black, and 1 percent are of Chinese descent. The official language is Spanish.

1970 / 8.5 million
40% Rural
60% Urban

1985 / 10.1 million
31% Rural
69% Urban

2000 / 11.2 million
26% Rural
74% Urban

2006 / 11.4 million
24% Rural
76% Urban

Common Spanish Phrases

Here are a few words and phrases you might use in Cuba. Give them a try:

Spanish	English
Adios (a-dee-os)	Goodbye
Sí	Yes
No	No
No hablo español.	I don't speak Spanish.
Me llamo...	My name is...
Donde está...?	Where is...?
Guagua	Bus

▲ Cuban children wear outfits from around the world at a festival celebrating the many different cultures that are part of the Cuban way of life.

Population Map

Cuban Homes

Cuban families are traditionally large. People cannot afford to build new houses, so children, parents, grandparents, and even great-grandparents often all live under one roof. Most families rent a few rooms in one of the apartment blocks that have been built since the 1960s. Large houses from colonial times are shared by several families. In the countryside, many people live in huts.

▲ A number of families share this old colonial palace in Havana.

▼ A family of farmers stand outside their *bohio*, a wooden house with a roof made from palm leaves.

Getting Around

Life in Cuba is affected by the country's politics, which have isolated it from the United States. The ban on trade with U.S. companies has made many things scarce. Gas is often in short supply, which brings public transportation to a halt. It's impossible to know if the bus or train will be running to get people to school or work. When the buses do run, they are often overcrowded.

A MIXTURE OF BELIEFS

Like other communist states, Cuba has no official religion. A few Cubans still practice Catholicism, which was brought to Cuba by the Spanish. Many more Cubans follow a faith named Santería. Santería was developed by slaves who wanted to practice African religions. The Spanish banned such beliefs and forced the slaves to convert, so the slaves disguised their old religions by blending them with elements of Christianity. Orishas, the gods of Santería, have become blended with Catholic saints. For example Ochun, the goddess of love, is closely linked to the Virgin Mary.

▲ A Santería altar in a home in Havana. A picture of the revolutionary leader Che Guevara has been included among the objects used in worship.

Cubans have many other ways to get around, including horse-drawn carts, bicycles, and even rickshaws. There are a few automobiles—collectors' items that are often over 50 years old. Many Cubans walk or make longer journeys by hitching rides. Truck drivers are usually happy to give lifts.

Food Rationing

Food is also scarce—even basics such as bread, eggs, and vegetables are often missing from stores.

▼ People travel through the old city of Trinidad in a horse-drawn cart, a way of getting around that requires no gasoline.

VINTAGE CARS

Cuba has been called "the world's greatest car museum." Vintage American cars from the 1940s and '50s, such as Cadillacs, Chevrolets, and Pontiacs, are sometimes seen on the streets. Car enthusiasts come from all over the world to admire the classic designs with their tail fins and gleaming chrome. The cars were imported from the United States before the 1959 revolution. The later ban on trade between the United States and Cuba prevented Cubans from getting spare parts, so they had to become experts at repairing their beloved cars. They use homemade parts or parts designed for Russian cars.

▲ A vintage car from the 1940s parked in a Cuban street. Cubans call the cars *cacharros*, which means "old pots."

Since the 1960s, food has been rationed—shared out so every person gets the same amount. No one has extra, but no one starves either. After a delivery of food, people may wait for hours to get their portion.

With so few ingredients to work with, cooks have to be inventive. Their recipes are simple but tasty, blending Spanish and Caribbean styles. A common dish is black beans and rice, which is often served with plantains. Meat and fish are mainly served on special occasions. Most meals end with a piece of fruit.

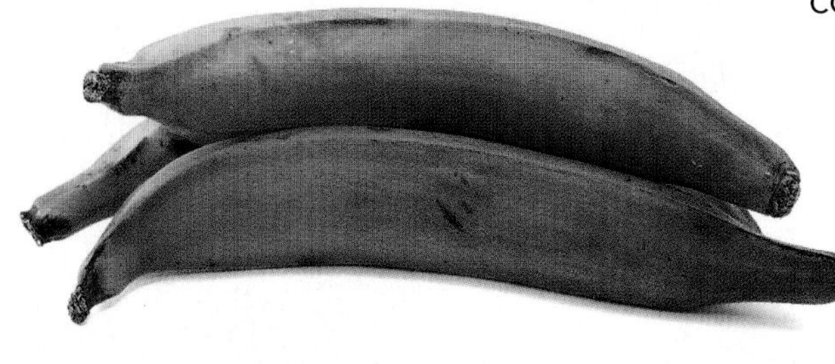

▼ **Plantains are a type of hard banana that taste like a cross between a banana and a potato when they are cooked.**

▲ **Primary school students dressed in red and white uniforms hold a picture of Che Guevara. From a young age, Cubans are encouraged to admire the leaders of the revolution.**

Going to School

Schooling and childcare are very important to Cuba's government. Before the revolution, many Cuban children had to leave school and work to support their families. Once in power, Fidel Castro launched a campaign to educate all Cubans. Today Cuba has a higher share of people who can read and write than any other Latin American or Caribbean country.

Schooling is free, and all children must attend between the ages of six and 14, with six years at primary school and three at high school. High-school students take basic courses in science, math, geography, Spanish, English, history, and art. Everyone studies the same subjects—and everyone wears the same uniform. Primary-school students all wear red, and high-school students dress in yellow.

If students want to enter higher education, they stay at high school for another three years. College education is free, and students can choose from more than 40 universities and technical colleges. The colleges offer useful subjects such as engineering.

The Arts

The Cuban government supports the arts, and even small towns have a cultural center for exhibitions and performances. Cuba has a reputation for painting and literature—and for being one of the world's most musical nations. Cubans make music everywhere, either on the street or in their local *casa de la trova* (music club). Guitars, double-basses, and trumpets are the most common instruments—but what

NATIONAL HOLIDAYS

In addition to national holidays, many religious festivals such as Catholic saints' days are also celebrated in Cuba.

January 1	New Year's Day and Liberation Day, celebrating the revolution in 1959
May 1	International Workers' Day
July 26	National Rebellion Day commemorates Castro's attack on the Moncada Barracks, Santiago de Cuba, in 1953. This marked the beginning of the revolution.
October 10	Anniversary of the start of the First War of Independence in 1868

▲ Cubans celebrate National Rebellion Day in July.

◀ **Musicians perform traditional son music in Havana. Son is dance music that combines lively rhythms with classical guitar playing.**

makes Cuban music so popular is the catchy rhythms of the bongos, maracas, and castanets. The main musical form is *son*, which combines Spanish and African influences.

Like Cuban music, Cuban dances have spread around the world. In the 1890s, dancers in Havana invented the rumba, a complex dance done with quick steps and swaying hips. By the 1940s, Cubans had developed new dances from rumba, including the mambo, the cha-cha, and salsa.

Sporting Nation

Cubans love all sports, but their favorite is baseball, which arrived from the United States

▼ **The national Cuban baseball team practices in Havana's Estadio Latinoamericano.**

in the 1860s. Teams from each province of the island take part in the National Series, which runs from November to March. Cubans are very proud of their national team. It is among the strongest in the world. In a remarkable run from 1987 to 1996, the Cuban team won 93 out of 94 international games. In the 2006 World Baseball Classic, it beat the United States, coming in second after Japan.

Boxing, soccer, volleyball, and basketball are also popular. The government supports sports and makes sure that children with athletic talent go to special schools to develop their skills. In recent years, Cuba has produced several world champions, such as long-jumper Iván Pedrosa (1972–). In the 1991 Pan-American Games, held in Havana, Cuba won 140 gold medals—more than any other country in the competition.

Leisure Time

Cubans do not usually have much leisure time. Many people work

A SPORTS LEGEND

Cuba has produced scores of great baseball players. Among the greatest was Martin Dihigo (1906–1971). Known as "El Negro," Dihigo is said to have played like Babe Ruth and Satchel Paige rolled into one. He won fame as a pitcher but played all nine positions at some point in his career.

Born in Matanzas, east of Havana, Dihigo showed remarkable talent as a child. He turned professional at 17 and traveled to the United States. At the time, black players had to play in a blacks-only league. And Dihigo encountered racism in other forms while living in the United States. Nevertheless, his success there helped pave the way for later black players to play in the major leagues. In a total of 21 seasons, Dihigo batted over .300 ten times. He is among the few players to be elected to the Baseball Hall of Fame in three countries—Cuba, the United States, and Mexico.

two jobs. But when they get off work, Cubans know how to enjoy themselves. Going to the movies and watching TV are popular. The two TV channels are both run by the government, but their top-rated shows include soap operas with interesting story lines. People also spend a lot of time outside their homes. Children play baseball in the street, while adults play music, sing, or dance, or join a game of dominoes at a local café. Others take their fishing poles and head for the coast. A fish is a tasty addition to the food rations.

▲ **Cuban men relax by playing dominoes.**

▼ **Young men fish near Havana's El Morro Castle.**

Escaping the Past

HAVANA ON MARKET DAY is a riot of color and noise. Shoppers from all over the city crowd around stalls to buy fruit and vegetables. The bustling scene looks as if it has not changed for decades. In fact, markets were banned in Cuba for much of the time between the 1960s and 1990s.

After the revolution in 1959, most Cuban farms were run by the state. They sold their crops at a set price to the government and had nothing left to sell at market. Today, however, three-quarters of Cuba's farms are owned by groups of families, who work together. Each farm can sell a share of its crops in the local market. The changes in farming are one sign of a transformation taking place all over Cuba, as the country moves toward a modern economic system.

◄ Shoppers visit a busy market outside the cathedral in the center of Havana. For many years after the revolution, markets like this were not allowed in Cuba.

A PEOPLE'S GOVERNMENT

Cuba is divided into 14 provinces. The provinces are divided into a total of 170 municipalities. Each municipality is governed by an assembly, with members elected by local people. The municipal assemblies elect members to a provincial assembly. The system of government aims to give Cubans a major say in their community. (One municipality, the Isla de la Juventud (the Isle of Youth), is directly ruled by the government.)

Cuba has two currencies—and both have the same name. The main currency for everday use is the peso. To buy luxury goods from overseas, Cubans must change their regular money into convertible pesos. One convertible peso is worth the same as one U.S. dollar. Convertible pesos are also used by tourists. The second currency allows the Cuban government to have total control over the money entering and leaving Cuba.

Trading Partners

After the revolution, 85 percent of Cuba's trade was with the Soviet Union. When the Soviet Union collapsed in 1990, Cuba had to find new trading partners. Cuba's chief exports are sugar, nickel, fish, fruits, and coffee. The main imports are fuel, food, machinery, and chemicals.

Country	Percentage Cuba exports
European Union	31.8%
Canada	20.6%
China	9.7%
All others combined	37.9%

Country	Percentage Cuba imports
European Union	27.4%
China	15.0%
Canada	8.7%
United States	8.5%
Mexico	4.8%
All others combined	35.6%

◀ A shopper uses Cuban pesos at a market stall. Convertible pesos must be used to buy foreign-made items.

Political Map
Gulf of Mexico
UNITED STATES
Straits of Florida
Cuban exiles, page 56
refugees, page 53
BAHAMAS
markets, page 3, 46, 48 and container ship, page 51 and drug store, page 54 and Castro, page 57
tourist hotels, page 57
TROPIC OF CANCER
Atlantic Ocean
CIUDAD DE LA HABANA
Havana
Mariel
Veradero
Matanzas
LA HABANA
MATANZAS
VILLA CLARA
PINAR DEL RÍO
Pinar del Río
Golfo de Batabanó
CIENFUEGOS
Cienfuegos
Santa Clara
SANCTI SPÍRITUS
Sancti Spíritus
CIEGO DE ÁVILA
Ciego de Ávila
Nueva Gerona
ISLA DE LA JUVENTUD
Yucatan Channel
sugar workers, page 55
Golfo de Ana María
Camagüey
CAMAGÜEY
LAS TUNAS
Las Tunas
Holguín
HOLGUÍN
bread rations, page 51
Caribbean Sea
Golfo de Guacanayabo
Bayamo
GRANMA
SANTIAGO DE CUBA
Santiago de Cuba
GUANTÁNAMO
Guantánamo
Windward Passage
U.S. NAVAL BASE GUANTANAMO BAY
Cayman Islands (U.K.)
JAMAICA
HAITI
MAP KEY
National capital
Provincial capital
Other city
0 miles 100
0 km 100
24°N
22°N
20°N
18°N
84°W
82°W
80°W
78°W
76°W
74°W

Friends and Enemies

Since 1959, Cubans have been living with the effects of their revolution. From the 1960s to the late 1980s, Fidel Castro's government maintained close ties with the Soviet Union and other communist nations. The Soviet Union sent aid to Cuba and was its main trading partner, supplying fuel and machinery in return for Cuban sugar. The United States remained hostile to Cuba, especially when Castro sent money and weapons to help rebel armies in Latin America, Africa, and the Middle East.

In the late 1980s, a major shift in world politics greatly affected Cuba. One by one, the communist governments of eastern Europe crumbled. In 1991,

HOW THE GOVERNMENT WORKS

Cuba is a socialist state run by the Cuban Communist Party, the *Partido Comunista de Cuba* (PCC). All Cubans 16 and over can vote in elections, but the PCC is the only legal party. Every member of the government is a member of the party. Cubans also vote for the 609 deputies of the National Assembly of People's Power. Not all deputies represent the PCC, but elected politicians have little say in Cuba. The full National Assembly only sits twice a year. Most laws are made by the Council of State, which is made up of 31 deputies appointed from the assembly. Fidel Castro is president of the Council of State, the first secretary of the PCC, and commander-in-chief of the armed forces. As well as being president, Castro is also prime minister of the Council of Ministers, which runs the country. The People's Supreme Court is the highest court in Cuba. Supreme Court judges are elected by the National Assembly.

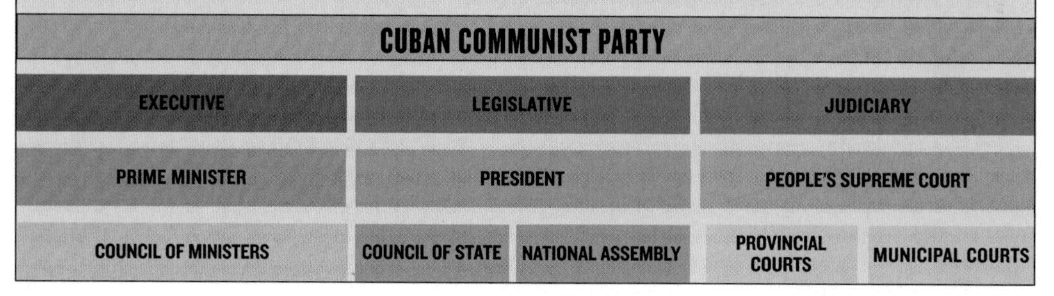

the Soviet Union broke up. The flow of aid and trade stopped abruptly. Without Soviet help, Cuba entered a deep economic crisis. Fuel and machinery became very scarce, and many Cuban factories had to close because they lacked raw materials.

▲ A ship leaves Havana in the 1980s carrying sugar and other produce to the Soviet Union.

▼ Cubans collect bread rations during hard times in the 1990s.

The Special Period

One of the worst problems facing Cuba after the collapse of the Soviet Union was a lack of food. To prevent starvation, the government announced emergency measures, known as the Special Period. Beginning in 1991, clothing and other products became rationed, and food rations were decreased. For example, people had a bread ration of just one roll

per day. There were ways around the restrictions. Although it was illegal, Cubans with U.S. dollars sent from abroad could buy what they wanted in secret.

The government made a few changes to solve its economic problems, including the reorganization of Cuba's farms. In 1993, the government began for the first time to encourage foreigners to invest in Cuba and to visit as tourists. Money from overseas, particularly U.S. dollars, could be used to buy the things Cuba needed to import. Castro built new trading links with Canada, the European Union, and China, as well as with Latin American countries. Venezuela, for example, became Cuba's chief supplier of oil. Cubans were able to start small businesses, such as shops and restaurants, so they could make more money for the country.

INDUSTRY AND MINING

This map shows the location of Cuba's mines and industrial centers. The main centers of manufacturing are large port cities such as Havana. Many of the sugar mills are located inland, in places such as Camagüey. The country's mines are in the east. Most are nickel mines. Cuba has about one-third of the world's nickel supply.

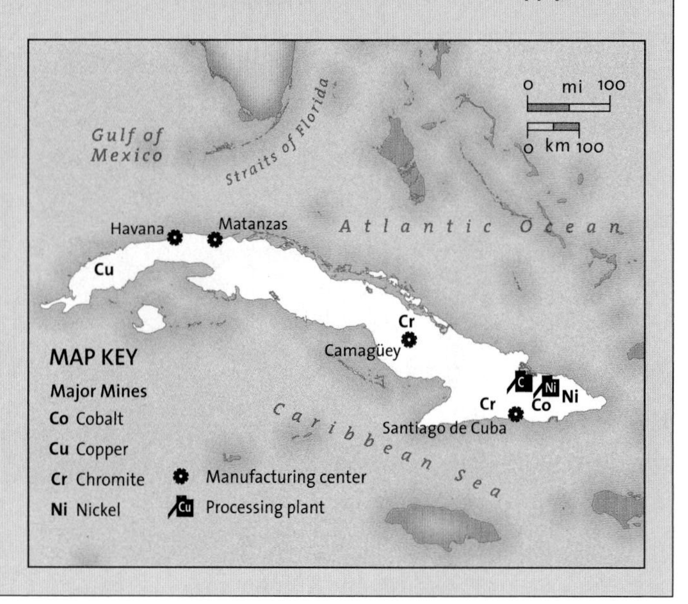

Refugees

In the years immediately after the 1959 revolution, 200,000 Cubans left the island. Most settled in the United States, although many also went to Spanish-speaking nations, such as Mexico. At first, the United States welcomed the refugees. As large numbers

continued to arrive, however, they added to tensions between the two nations. Over the summer of 1980, 125,000 Cubans left the port of Mariel bound for Florida in a migration known as the Mariel Boatlift. In 1994, another large migration took place, with many Cubans crossing the Straits of Florida on rafts made from barrels and old pieces of wood. Many of the refugees drowned. Eventually, the United States agreed to accept 20,000 people from Cuba each year. In return, Cuba promised to do more to halt the flow of refugees.

▲ Cuban refugees cross the Straits of Florida on rafts in 1994. Most refugees at the time were picked up by the U.S. Coast Guard and sent to a camp at the Guantánamo Bay naval base. Eventually they were allowed to enter the United States. A total of 1.2 million Cubans now live abroad.

Cash-Crop Economy

About 20 percent of Cubans work on farms or as fishers. The most important crops are sugar and coffee, which can be sold abroad. The government also encourages farmers to grow produce for the home

▲ **Customers wait in line at a drugstore in Havana. Although medical supplies are scarce, most of Cuba's people live into their late seventies—just as long as an average American citizen.**

market. Cuba's farms produce all the rice, corn, beans, vegetables, and fruits the country needs. However, the wheat used to make flour for bread and other baked goods must be imported.

Farmers raise cattle, pigs, and chickens for their meat, milk, and eggs. Fish is an important part of the diet. Fishing boats operate in the Caribbean and in the Atlantic Ocean. The most important catches include tuna and shellfish such as lobsters and shrimp.

Working in Industry

About one-third of Cubans work in industries like manufacturing and mining. Mines produce chromium, cobalt, iron, nickel, and copper ore. The country has a few oil wells, but it still needs to import virtually all of its oil. One of Cuba's most important industries was also its first: sugar production. There are dozens of *ingenios* (sugar mills) operating on the island. Cuba is also famous for its cigars and rum.

Most Cubans work in service industries. They include teachers, bus and train drivers, and people who work for the government. Many work in health care, including about 71,000 doctors. That is one doctor for every 160 patients—more than most countries, including the United States. There is such a high number because it is free to train as a doctor in Cuba if you get good grades.

Since the reforms of the 1980s, tourism has become a booming industry in Cuba. Most visitors come from Canada and Europe. In 1996, tourism became Cuba's biggest industry, earning more money than sugar for the first time. Nearly two million tourists visit each year and spend more than $2 billion.

Looking to the Future

The revolutionary government has proved a mixed blessing for Cubans. Wealth is now more evenly

MAKING SUGAR

Sugar has been at the heart of Cuba's economy since the Spanish introduced the crop in the 16th century. Long stalks of sugarcane are cut each year between December and June. Machines cut the cane on the plains, but in the hills workers need to hack it down with machetes. In the late 19th century, a rail network was built to carry the cane from the plantations to the sugar mills. It is still in use today. At the mills, the cane is washed and crushed to extract the juice, which is processed to make a dark syrup. The syrup is heated to make grains of brown sugar. Other products made from sugarcane include a rich, honey-like syrup called molasses and Cuban rum. Even the plant's fibers are used as animal feed.

▲ Workers shovel sugar that has been delivered by train to the port of Cienfugos.

distributed among the population. The position of women and black people has improved. In addition, Cubans enjoy health care and educations that are as good as those of much wealthier nations. Many Cubans are proud of such successful social programs.

On the downside, Cuba's economy remains undeveloped. Wages and living standards are very low compared to other North American countries. Basic necessities such as electricity and clean water, which are taken for granted in many other places,

DON'T BUY CUBAN

Since 1962, most trade between the United States and Cuba has been illegal. The United States imposed a trade ban after Castro seized U.S. businesses in Cuba, including oil refineries. Nations from the Organization of American States (OAS) also banned trade with Cuba. However, while OAS lifted its ban in 1975, the U.S. ban remains in place. It was strengthened in the 1990s under pressure from Cubans living in the United States. U.S. firms can only export medicines and certain foods to Cuba.

The ban was originally intended to weaken Castro's government to make it easier for the Cuban people to overthrow it. It failed in its purpose. Many people have come to disagree with the ban, including the United Nations. They think that its only real impact is to make life more difficult for ordinary Cubans.

▲ **Cuban exiles living in Miami, Florida, protest against the Castro-led government in their home country.**

remain scarce in Cuba. Cubans also have very little personal freedom. For example, they cannot use the Internet without permission from the authorities. People who speak out against the government have been put in prison or exiled (sent abroad).

▲ **Luxury hotels fill a long, beach-lined peninsula at Varadero.**

Time for Change?

In 2006, Fidel Castro had been in power for 47 years —longer than any of the world's other leaders. However, in July 2006, he suffered a serious stomach illness. He was too sick to join the nation's celebrations of his eightieth birthday. Vice President Raúl Castro, Fidel's brother, took charge of the government and the armed forces when the president's health failed. Raúl is five years younger than his brother. If he takes over permanently, he may keep Cuba on its revolutionary course for a few more years. However, at some point soon, the Castro era will end. When this happens, change may come quickly, and Cuba may take a very different direction, perhaps toward greater political freedom and a more open economy. Whatever happens, the Cuban people are likely to continue to enjoy life with their usual optimism and good humor.

▼ **Fidel Castro is one of the last communist leaders in the world.**

Add a Little Extra to Your Country Report!

If you are assigned to write a report about Cuba, you'll want to include basic information about the country, of course. The Fast Facts chart on page 8 will give you a good start. The rest of the book will give you the details you need to create a full and up-to-date paper or PowerPoint presentation. But what can you do to make your report more fun than anyone else's? If you use your imagination and dig a bit deeper into some of the topics introduced in this book, you're sure to come up with information that will make your report unique!

>*Flag*

Perhaps you could explain the history of Cuba's flag, and the meanings of its colors and symbol. Go to **www.crwflags.com/fotw/flags** for more information.

>*National Anthem*

How about downloading Cuba's national anthem, and playing it for your class? At **www.nationalanthems.info** you'll find what you need, including the words to the anthem, plus sheet music for it. Simply pick "C" and then "Cuba" from the list on the left-hand side of the screen, and you're on your way.

>*Time Difference*

If you want to understand the time difference between Cuba and where you are, this Web site can help: **www.worldtimeserver.com**. Just pick "Cuba" from the list on the left. If you called Cuba right now, would you wake whomever you are calling from their sleep?

>*Currency*

Another Web site will convert your money into Cuban pesos, the currency used in Cuba. You'll want to know how much money to bring if you're ever lucky enough to travel to Cuba: **www.xe.com/ucc**.

>*Weather*

Why not check the current weather in Cuba? It's easy—simply go to **www.weather.com** to find out if it's sunny or cloudy, warm or cold in Cuba right this minute! Pick "World" from the headings at the top of the page. Then search for Cuba. Click on any city you like. Be sure to click on the tabs below the weather report for Sunrise/Sunset information, Weather Watch, and Business Travel Outlook, too. Scroll down the page for the 36-hour Forecast and a satellite weather map. Compare your weather to the weather in the Cuban city you chose. Is this a good season, weather-wise, for a person to travel to Cuba?

>*Miscellaneous*

Still want more information? Simply go to National Geographic's One-Stop Research site at **http://www.nationalgeographic.com/onestop**. It will help you find maps, photos and art, articles and information, games and features that you can use to jazz up your report.

Glossary

Bohio a small traditional wooden house in the countryside of Cuba. Most bohios have a roof made from dried palm leaves.

Carnival in Cuba, a party that takes place in the streets of a town or city during a summer holiday. People dance, play music, and take part in processions dressed in bright costumes.

Causeway a long bridge that crosses the sea to connect an island to the mainland. Some causeways are covered by water at high tide.

Colony a region that is ruled by a nation located somewhere else in the world. Settlers from that distant country take the land from the region's original inhabitants.

Communism a system of government where a single political party rules a country with the job of ensuring that wealth is shared equally among all the people in the country. Cuba is one of the few communist countries left in the world.

Culture a collection of beliefs, traditions, and styles that belongs to people living in a certain part of the world.

Dictator a leader who has complete control over a country and does not have to be elected or re-elected to office regularly.

Embargo a ban on trade between nations.

Habitat a part of the environment that is suitable for certain plants and animals.

Hemisphere one half of a sphere, or globe. Earth is generally divided into the Western and Eastern Hemisphere. Cuba is in the Western Hemisphere.

Lagoon a shallow lake that is close to, and often connected to, the sea.

Mogotes an unusual type of steep rocky hill located in western Cuba.

New World a term used to describe North and South America. These continents were given this name by settlers from Europe, which they termed the Old World.

Old World a term used to describe Europe, Africa, and Asia.

Orisha a god or spirit that is worshiped as part of Cuba's Santería religion.

Peninsula a narrow piece of land that is surrounded by water on three sides. The word means "almost island" in Latin.

Plumage a bird's covering of feathers.

Refugee a person fleeing from his or her home country to escape a war, poverty, or other dangers.

Revolutionary a person who wishes to replace a country's government using violence.

Soviet Union a large empire of communist states that existed between 1917 and 1990. The union included countries such as Russia, Ukraine, and Armenia, which are now independent from each other.

Species a type of organism; animals or plants in the same species look similar and can only breed successfully among themselves.

Tropic of Cancer a line that marks the northernmost point of Earth's warm tropical zone.

United Nations (UN) an international organization that includes most of the countries of the world. The UN is where the world's governments discuss the world's problems and figure out how to work together to solve them.

Bibliography

Campbell, Kumari. *Cuba in Pictures*. Minneapolis, MN: Lerner Publications Co., 2005.

Dunn, John M. *Life in Castro's Cuba*. San Diego, CA: Lucent Books, 2004.

http://www.cubagob.cu/ingles/default.htm (government Web site)

http://www.miami.com/mld/miamiherald/news/world/cuba/ (news from Cuba supplied by the *Miami Herald* newspaper in Florida)

http://www.state.gov/r/pa/ei/bgn/2886.htm (general information from the U.S. State Department)

Further Information

National Geographic Articles

Allen, Thomas B. "Cuba's Golden Past." National Geographic (July 2001): 74-91.

Barr, Brady and Margaret Zackowitz. "Chasing Down the Cuban Crocodile." National Geographic World (July 2001): 14.

Web sites to explore

More fast facts about Cuba, from the CIA (Central Intelligence Agency): https://www.cia.gov/cia/publications/factbook/geos/cu.html

Want to know more about the Zapata Biosphere Reserve, the home of the Cuban crocodile? Information from the United Nations Educational, Scientific and Cultural Organization (UNESCO) is at: http://www2.unesco.org/mab/br/brdir/directory/biores.asp?code=CUB+05&mode=all

Everything you need to know about the extraordinary career of Cuban leader Fidel Castro. Click on this biography from PBS: http://www.pbs.org/wgbh/amex/castro/peopleevents/p_castro.html

Interested in the Taíno, Cuba's original inhabitants? El Museo's art and culture site is one of the best places to learn more: http://www.ns.ec.gc.ca/wildlife/index.html

See, hear

There are many ways to get a taste of life in Cuba, such as movies, music CDs, magazines, or TV shows. You might be able to locate these:

Buena Vista Social Club (1999)
This movie about Cuban music by U.S. director Wim Wenders is full of great performances by traditional musicians. There is a music CD of the same name.

Prisma
This English-language magazine is published in Havana every month. If anyone you know goes to Cuba, ask them to bring you a copy.

East of Havana (2006)
This movie, produced by the star Charlize Theron, is about rappers in Cuba.

I Am Cuba (1964)
This movie was made by the Soviets and shows Cuba as it used to be.

The Rough Guide to Cuban Music (2001)
A book of songs by some of the island's best musicians.

Index

Credits

Picture Credits

Front Cover—Spine: Rafael Martin-Gaitero/Sutterstock; Top: Nicolas Reynard/NGIC; Lo far left: Claudia Daut/Reuters/ Corbis; Lo left: David Alan Harvey/NGIC; Lo right: Medford Taylor/ NGIC; Lo far right: Steve Winter/NGIC.

Interior—Corbis: Archive Iconografico, S.A.: 27 up; Bettmann: 31 up, 32 lo, 33 up; Robert Duyos 56 center; Bob Krist: 43 up; Tim Page: 55 lo; Reuters: 53 up; Kurt Stier: 29 up; Les Stone: 48 center; Nik Wheeler: 3 right, 46-47; Getty Images: MLB Photos: 44 up; NG Image Collection: Ira Block: 2-3, 22-23, 24 up, 45 lo; David Alan Harvey: 3 left, 10 up, 28 lo, 34-35, 36 up, 38 up, 38 lo, 41 up, 42 lo, 51 lo, 57 up, 57 lo; Taylor S. Kennedy: 5 up, 39 up, 40 up, 54 up, 59 up; Mattias Klum: 18 lo; Pete McBride: 45 up; Steve Raymer: 30 lo; Brian J, Skerry: 19 lo; James L. Stanfield: 51 up; James A. Sugar: 26 lo; Medford Taylor: TP, 2 left, 6-7, 39 lo, 43 lo; Steve Winter: 2 right, 11 lo, 12 centre, 13 up, 14-15, 16 up, 19 up, 20 up; Photo Researchers, Inc.: James A. Hancock: 21 up; Shutterstock: Nina Shannon: 40 lo.

For more information, please call 1-800-NGS-LINE (647-5463) or write to the following address:

NATIONAL GEOGRAPHIC SOCIETY
1145 17th Street N.W.
Washington, D.C. 20036-4688 U.S.A.

Visit the Society's Web site at **www.nationalgeographic.com**

Library of Congress Cataloging-in-Publication Data available on request
ISBN: 978-1-4263-0057-8

Printed in Belgium

Series design by Jim Hiscott.
The body text is set in Avenir; Knockout.
The display text is set in Matrix Script.

Front Cover—Top: A street at dusk in Trinidad; Low Far Left: A vintage car in a street in Havana; Low Left: Young Cuban screech owls peer from their nest in the Cienaga de Zapata Biosphere Reserve; Low Right: Flags at a rally to celebrate the Cuban revolution; Low Far Right: Palm trees on the beach at Santa Maria del Mar

Page 1—A woman in a formal white dress passes vintage cars in downtown Havana; Icon image on spine, Contents page, and throughout: License plate of Cuban vintage car

Produced through the worldwide resources of the National Geographic Society

John M. Fahey, Jr., *President and Chief Executive Officer,* Gilbert M. Grosvenor, *Chairman of the Board;* Nina D. Hoffman, *Executive Vice President, President of Book Publishing Group*

National Geographic Staff for this book

Nancy Laties Feresten, *Vice President, Editor-in-Chief of Children's Books*
Bea Jackson, *Director of Design and Illustration*
David M. Seager, *Art Director*
Virginia Koeth, *Project Editor*
Lori Epstein, *Illustrations Editor*
Stacy Gold, *Nadia Hughes, Illustrations Research Editors*
Carl Mehler, *Director of Maps*
Priyanka Lamichhane, *Assistant Editor*
R. Gary Colbert, *Production Director*
Lewis R. Bassford, *Production Manager*
Maryclare Tracy, Nicole Elliott, *Manufacturing Managers*

Brown Reference Group plc. Staff for this book

Volume Editor: Tom Jackson
Designer: Dave Allen
Picture Manager: Becky Cox
Maps: Martin Darlinson
Artwork: Darren Awuah
Index: Kay Ollerenshaw
Senior Managing Editor: Tim Cooke
Design Manager: Sarah Williams
Children's Publisher: Anne O'Daly
Editorial Director: Lindsey Lowe

About the Author

JEN GREEN received a doctorate from the University of Sussex, United Kingdom, in 1982. She worked in publishing for 15 years and is now a full-time writer who has written more than 150 books for children on natural history, geography, the environment, history, and other subjects.

About the Consultants

DR. DAMIÁN FERNÁNDEZ is Director of the Cuban Research Institute, Professor of International Relations, and Vice Provost of the Biscayne Bay campus of Florida International University in Miami. Among other publications, he is the author of *Cuba and the Politics of Passion* (2000), the co-editor of *Cuba, the Elusive Nation: Reinterpretations of National Identity* (2000), and the editor of *Cuba Transnational* (2005). His research interests include Cuban politics; informality, emotions, and the politics of civil society; Latin America's international relations; and Hispanics and U.S. foreign policy.

DR. ALEJANDRO DE LA FUENTE is an associate professor of Latin American and Caribbean History at the University of Pittsburgh. He specializes in Atlantic history, the study of slavery, and race relations. He is the author of *A Nation for All: Race, Inequality, and Politics in Twentieth-Century Cuba* (2001).

Time Line of Cuban History

B.C.

ca 1000 The Guanahatabey and Ciboney are living on Cuba by this time.

A.D.

ca 800 The Taino arrive from South America.

1400

1492 Christopher Columbus arrives in Cuba and claims it for Spain.

1500

1511 Diego de Velazquez leads the Spanish colonization of Cuba.

1526 As the African slave trade grows, Havana becomes a major port.

1600

1607 Havana becomes the capital of Cuba.

1700

1762 Spain enters the Seven Years' War against Great Britain. British forces capture Havana and open the port to trade with Great Britain.

1763 Spain regains control of Havana by the Treaty of Paris.

1795 Pinckney's Treaty establishes commercial relations between the U.S. and Spain.

1800

1819 The Adams-Onis Trea ty fomally renews commercial ties between the U.S. and Spain.

1868-78 Carlos Manuel de Céspedes begins the Ten Years' War for independence from Spain. The war ends with Spain promising Cuba more independence.

1886 Slavery is abolished in Cuba.

1892 José Martí founds the Cuban Revolutionary Party.

1895-98 José Martí leads a second war of independence.

1898 The Spanish-American War begins when Spain refuses American requests to leave Cuba. The war is ended by the Treaty of Paris, and Spain grants Cuba independence.

1899-1901 A U.S. military goverment takes power in Cuba.

1900

1901 The Platt Amendment to the Cuban Constitution gives the U.S. the right to intervene in Cuba's internal affairs and keep a naval base on the island, while forbidding Cuba from signing treaties or making financial agreements with other countries.

1902 Cuba becomes independent with Tomas Estrada Palma as president, but the U.S. keeps its right to intervene in Cuban affairs.

1906-09 Jose Miguel Gomez leads a rebellion that leads to Estrada's resignation and a U.S. occupation of Cuba.

1909 Jose Miguel Gomez is elected president in U.S.-supervised elections.

1924 Gerado Machado rises to power; he later establishes a dictatorship.